ATAP, AW

All Things Are Possible, Anywhere

ATAP, AW

All Things Are Possible, Anywhere

Debra Cox

GLORIOUS WORKS PUBLISHING
Upper Darby, Pennsylvania

Copyright © 2020 by Debra Cox

All rights reserved. This book or any portion thereof may not be reproduced or used ina any manner whatsoever without the express written permission of the publisher except for the use of brief quotations in a book review or scholarly journal.

First Printing: 2020

ISBN: 978-1-7335565-7-6

Unless otherwise indicated, all Scripture quotations are taken from the King James Version (KJV): King James Version, public domain. Scripture quotations marked MSG are taken from *THE MESSAGE*, copyright © 1993, 2002, 2018 by Eugene H. Peterson. Used by permission of NavPress. All rights reserved.

> Glorious Works Publishing
> 201 Bywood Ave. #2214
> Upper Darby, PA 19082
> www.gloriousworkspublishing.com

Special discounts are available on bulk purchases. For details, contact publisher at admin@gloriousworkspublishing.com.

Glorious Works Publishing can bring authors to your live events. For more information or to book an event, contact Glorious Works Publishing at admin@gloriousworkspublishing.com or visit our website at www.gloriousworkspublishing.com.

Publisher's Cataloging-In-Publication Data
(Prepared by The Donohue Group, Inc.)

Names: Cox, Debra, author.
Title: ATAP, AW : all things are possible, anywhere / Debra Cox.
Other Titles: All things are possible, anywhere
Description: Upper Darby, PA : Glorious Works Publishing, [2020]
Identifiers: ISBN 9781733556576
Subjects: LCSH: Self-actualization (Psychology)--Religious aspects--
 Christianity. | Change (Psychology)--Religious aspects--Christianity. | Goal
 (Psychology)--Religious aspects--Christianity. | Self-help techniques.
Classification: LCC BV4598.2 .C69 2020 | DDC 248.4--dc23

Contents

Acknowledgments.. 2

Introduction 4

Chapter One
Living in Vault..7

Chapter Two
Living in the Borough of Lackton.................... 15

Chapter Three
The Status of Staticus................................... 25

Chapter Four
The Town of Comfort Zone 35

Chapter Five
The Town of Fearford..................................... 43

Chapter Six
Bordering ATAP 51

Chapter Seven
Mind AveNews... 59

About the Author 76

Acknowledgments

There are so many people to thank for this incredible accomplishment. I remember listening with awe to the late Rev. James L Dandridge of Mt. Pisgah AME Church when I was a teenager, making mental notes of how he crafted words in his sermons, hoping one day I could gather thoughts like that to paper.

Then there's my English teacher who taught at Lincoln College Preparatory School; I learned so much from her. Then while taking an English composition class at Wilberforce University, my professor gave me a great compliment regarding writing a movie review. The paper was about me pretending to be a movie critic reviewing a movie; she told me it was one of the best articles she ever read.

As I got older, I began creating greeting cards people seemed to like, and let's not forget the many newsletters I wrote for the choir at Beulah Baptist Church. All my 'readers' seemed to like the ideas, and many encouraged me to keep writing. I thank them all.

To my son Steve, who continually inspires me, and countless friends who tell me to continue, I say thank you all. But the most prominent acknowledgment has to be to the One who made it all happen—the One who created me.

Thank you, God, for putting the gift of writing in me. Thank you for trusting and believing in me, encouraging me to get this first book completed. You never gave up on me when I thought I allowed too much time to escape, when I thought I was too old to be creative, or when I let my struggles get the best of me. But you saw through all that and gifted me anyway, and for that, I have many thanks. As you have given to me, I return to You. You know how I love helping others find their way in life, and You have helped me find mine.

New ideas for my next offering are circling in my head, and I hope I allow them to breathe into reality, just as You have allowed me to open myself to the possibility that this could happen. This book is my way of acknowledging You as You have done for me.

Thank you,

Debra

Introduction

When I thought of writing this book, butterflies began to visit my stomach as I became nervous and excited at the same time. Before starting to write, I knew an enlightening change was to begin. Among other descriptions, words like discipline, continuance, and creativity came to mind. But the most significant interpretation that resonated was the word change.

This word would develop my dream of being a published author, a thought I've had for decades. This word, if allowed to unfold within me, would deny me from watching reruns of my favorite television show, Fixer Upper, on HGTV (sorry Chip and Joanna). This word would envelop an inward drive to enable me to stay on the course of writing at least 450 words a day. This word would eliminate the act of standing still and instead of moving at the speed of thought, evolving from my head and filling my blank computer screen. I just had to believe it could happen, and it had to begin with taking a trip to ATAP, AW. Where is that place? I'm so glad you asked.

ATAP, AW means All Things Are Possible, Anywhere, and I hope it is where we all go at some time in our lives. This place should not be a temporary destination. It's not a vacation spot to relax and get away from life's chaos. It is an atmosphere where one realizes empowerment, an environment where ideas are discovered and carried out. It is a municipality where one can actualize their thoughts and exercise bold steps. Sadly, many do not go there. Instead, they decide to stay permanently in their present location from a mental standpoint.

In our minds, there are cities we visit, towns where nothing moves, and this book hopes to define the vast dungeons of stagnancy and complacency, a critical indication that one is not experiencing life in ATAP, AW. Mentally, one may live for years without deciding to progress. While one wants to go to a place of positivity, the problem hinges around the fear of stepping out. They have to choose to get out of their comfort zones and eventually to ATAP, AW.

If change does not begin, the result leads to stagnancy, inactiveness, being static, and feeling incapable of dreams becoming a reality. The idea of launching into the deep appears promising, but quickly becomes fleeting, and is quickly dismissed because one is unsure of the possibility of accomplishing it. Have you felt the same?

Launching into the deep takes some serious action for anyone wanting to make life changes. A beginning, in and of itself, can be scary, but it is well worth the trip to venture there. It is the action of being real with yourself while deciding to put the work in that makes dreams come alive. It is going beyond just thinking, and instead, moving forward to causing the 'it' to happen and become a reality.

What are your goals? What have you thought about doing? Has God been continuously pricking your mind to do it, but you dismiss any chance of birthing it into reality? Take a journey with me and see how this resonates with you. If it does, I hope that this book will help challenge you to not only visit ATAP, AW, but to reside there forever.

1. Write a list of goals you hope to achieve.
2. How do you define launching into the deep?
3. When you think of working on a goal, what concerns do you have?
4. How would your life be if you launched into the deep?

Chapter One
Living in Vault

I have pages and pages of ideas to write about, complete with titles per impression. I love creating plans, thinking of how to develop them, in hopes of giving each one the legs of action. The more I would think about the love of creating ideas, the more I started to wonder if that was all I liked to do, and not going beyond that.

When this thought entered my brainwaves, it stunned me, wondering if this described me. Perhaps this, though, had some validity, loving to create ideas, preferring not to go further. Going further would lead me to the path of actually doing something with the concept, giving it more than a thought, but acting upon it. Pushing past my initial idea would involve extending myself into the unknown, which, for me, is a bit terrifying. The unknown is, well, unknown, which leaves me fearful of how to continue with the thought, the formulation of something new that is developing in my mind. Let's call the 'something' the idea, defined as an:

Individual

Design (that's)

Enacted (by some sort of)

Activity or action.

One of the ideas that entered my mind and journeyed through to ATAP is sitting right before your eyes, this book, *ATAP, AW*. Such mental activity requires discovery, identification, and clarification to have a chance to be established in the realm of reality.

First, let's define reality. Though the Oxford Dictionary of English had many definitions, these were the two that fit the context I am trying to establish:

The state of things as they actually exist, as opposed to an idealistic or notional idea of them

A thing that exists in fact, having previously only existed in one's mind

Based on these two definitions, an idea may not be a reality yet, but it is aching to get there. When one creates an idea, it involves the following elements:

Discovery

For me, this is the fun part, as it has a creative feature. An idea trickles into the brain and causes one to wonder; could this happen? Discovery brings the excitement of delving into the realm of mental possibilities, how it could work, what needs to happen to bring it into reality. Perhaps discovery is the natural part. There could be something you always have desired to do, and detection and acknowledgment of the thought is a good thing, as the idea forwards to another positive atmosphere called identification.

Identification

Identification can be a bit more involved. To identify with something is to associate with the idea and all its components. It is where the thought of the plan begins to formulate. It means to bring the concept out of the unknown, to a place where reality can unfold and take shape.

Chapter One: Living in Vault

To identify is to link up to it, associate to it. As someone associates with the idea, it is like taking the concept apart, further discovering the contents, which leads to idea clarification.

Clarification

You might already be asking yourself questions like, how is this going to happen? How can I maneuver my already hectic life to work on this idea and make it a factual existence? Perhaps developing a business plan for your idea of starting a business would help to make more explicit the specifics of how the business idea can become a reality. Having the concept creatively transform from the mind to syntax flow on paper not only empties the mind but brings together these three elements in hopes of moving closer to the idea happening.

Can you imagine the idea becoming excited, first being created, then running through your mind dreaming of becoming less of an ideology and more of an act that truly happens? But as there is a desire to being instrumental in resonating change, sometimes the idea is forced to take up residence in a place it may not want to live.

The title of this book is ATAP, AW, which means All Things Are Possible, Anywhere. ATAP, AW is where the *new* becomes *known*. It is where the unfamiliar becomes familiar, where knowledge is discovered, identified, and clarified. ATAP is a town where people come to transform themselves, as the idea undergoes a metamorphosis from the impossible to the possible. Creators flock there to write plays, books, poetry, music, creating a series of words that culminate beautiful and encouraging thoughts, creatively formulated to statements many need to read and hear. It is a place where others come to create inventions, design buildings, and so much more.

ATAP, AW

ATAP is a peaceful, lovely place to be, located in the state of AW or **A**ny**w**here, as ATAP can happen where one may not be expecting it. ATAP can occur in a dream, on a bus, plane, in a car while driving, in the quietness of one's home, in the stillness of the night. But frequently, these precious ideas get blindsided to another place called Raef, a place far different than ATAP, AW.

Raef is on the outskirts of ATAP. Raef is full of inhabitants that have **R**educed their **A**bility to **E**stablish **F**aith: faith in themselves, in others, in God. How is this place? Another good question you ask.

For one, it is an indicator you are not on a proper footing, a place that does not invite the positive. Imagine in the realm of the mind many cities formulate, where ideas reside. It is the choice of the person to place the idea in one of these cities. For example, a person could choose to place an idea in Raef.

Raef is like a holding pattern, similar to an airplane that circles its landing point, waiting for clearance to land at its destination. It is where many go to contemplate an idea, preferring not to permit it to land in an environment of reality. The majority of great ideas were on their way to ATAP but changed their destination to Raef. The person who put the idea in this town believes it to be the best place for it to reside. The city's motto is Raef: The Easy Place. And the mind prides itself on presenting the city as an engaging, friendly host to all that move in.

The idea travels to a section in the city called Vault. Vault is similar to the vault in a bank where customers rent a box to place their valuables under lock and key. That includes essential papers like stock, will, and the like. In this context, Vault is a mental place where the idea goes for safekeeping. Just like a bank customer reviews the contents of their safe deposit box, we mentally keep great ideas under wraps in the vault of our mind.

Chapter One: Living in Vault

In our quiet moments, we may mentally visit Vault, sitting on a bench and viewing the idea, taking it out to review, ensuring it's still there, only to tuck it back in the vault under lock and key. Vault is where ideas reside, enabling the person who placed it there to feel comfortable. Ideas can come with unresolved baggage, and in Vault, there is an abundance of storage that not only keeps the ideas but the baggage that goes along with them.

In Vault, when the idea awakens and pops up in a person's mind, the person (the owner of the idea) can quickly put the idea to sleep (at least for the time being). It seems the idea hasn't a care in the mental world, as living life in Raef is excellent, at least during the day when there is not much for the idea to do. The owner imagines living life this way is in the best interest of the idea, which doesn't have much to do.

But then comes the night.

When night comes, all is not silent. The residents (the ideas) try endlessly to slip out of Vault and to move. After all, the goal of the idea is to get to reality. At the same time, the owner of the concept attempts to keep it dormant and secure in its assigned area.

Though the idea is in Vault, which is within the region of Raef (a place devoid of faith), the ideas keep repeating, "We're still here. When will we become a reality? We started this journey to get to ATAP. Instead, you moved us to Raef, and we're stuck in Vault. Why do you keep doing this to us? We are the vision, a gift given to you, but you keep vaulting us up. What happened? You can keep reducing your ability to establish faith all you want, but realize this: we are **real.** We are the **actual evidence that God gave you.**"

A key indication your ideas are living in Vault is the thought keeps popping up. You may want to keep it for safekeeping, but because it keeps reminding you it is still in the recesses of your mind is an indication you need to act on it, yet you choose to do the opposite.

> *"The value of an idea lies in the using of it."*
> ***Thomas Edison***

> *"Ideas won't keep. Something must be done about them."* ***Alfred North Whitehead***

If an idea comes to you, tucking it away in Vault for safekeeping is not the best choice. I can attest to this line of thinking, as I have desired to write a book for years. My indicator of not living in ATAP was that my mind was full of confusion. Coming up with idea after idea while not doing anything about them was my way of living. Tucking them away in Vault was my choice, my thought process of mentally living in Raef, a decision, but not a good one. That was what I concluded about myself, thinking it was a good idea, not having the belief in myself that I could pull off writing a book.

Another indicator of having a mental vault is that while you are alive and experiencing life, you may not be enjoying it. There is a commercial that comes to mind. The man in the ad was talking to his financial advisor, who asked if he thought about starting his own business, and his reply was 'every day.' It wasn't that he did not have the idea of doing it, but it seemed he wasn't doing anything about it, hence the possibility of him tucking it away in Vault.

Do you daily think about what your dream life could be yet don't do anything about it, continuing to live a subpar life and not enjoying much? Chances are this section describes you, and you need to do something about it.

Chapter One: Living in Vault

Chapter Summary:

1. An **IDEA** is an **I**ndividual **D**esign (that's) **E**nacted (by some sort of) **A**ctivity or action.
2. The values of ideas don't mean much if kept in the locked safe of a mental vault.
3. Identify what you have been tucking away in the city of Vault.
4. Recall what you do when an idea continually pops in your head.
5. Ideas don't keep. Something must be done about them.
6. Choose to act on your ideas and enjoy life.

Chapter Two
Living in the Borough of Lackton

Do you feel like you're in a state of wanting to do something but sense a state of being deficient? When you think of going back to school, do you believe you are absent from having the skills necessary to obtain the degree? You may be living in the Borough of Lackton.

I am reminded of a story in the Bible that exemplifies a resident of Lackton all too well. Consider Moses from the book of Exodus. Perhaps Moses felt he was absent of many things to complete tasks God wanted him to finish.

Moses had to come out of his cocoon of living on the backside of Midian with his family. The children of Israel were under bondage in Egypt, and they cried out to God to be free. Showing favor to them, God chose Moses to be their leader in performing the task of bringing them from slavery to the Promised Land. Though this was God's plan, Moses wanted no part of it. Through their conversation, God presented the plan through identifying and clarifying His goal, including telling Pharoah to let His people go, and provided tools for Moses to use (like the staff) in the attempt to persuade Pharoah to free the children of Israel. But Moses had a presentation of his own, as recorded in the third chapter of Exodus.

"Who am I?"

"Who do you think I am that you would want me to do this?"

Perhaps the current of this question was pulsating so strong through Moses' mind that it caused him to ask God this question. Imagine the surprised expression on Moses' face when God presented His plan. Perhaps Moses thought of who God thought he was to even think of doing something like that. I am sure Moses thought what many of us believe when a great idea comes to mind. While Moses was concerned about his people in Egypt, it may not have been in his mind that he would free Israel. Maybe Israel's freedom was an idea Moses had tucked away in Vault. The critical thought in Moses' mind was this: God, regardless of what you say, I am unqualified, lacking the skills necessary to do as you propose.

Do you feel the same, one that does not recognize yourself as having the needed skills required to perform a task or goal successfully?

God answered that Moses was the chosen one, and He would be with him. It was as if God was saying, "Don't worry, Moses, I won't leave you hanging; you're the one who will represent Me to bring Israel out from the house of bondage. Oh, and something else: I got your back." But, it appears Moses wasn't so sure.

Have you thought of something you would be good at, but at the same time, you felt like Moses, who had a *'who am I' mentality*? How could *you* be the one that will stand in front of others to speak? How could *you* be successful in going back to school? How could *you* be the one to change careers and do something different at an age when you should be retiring? Like Moses, you could be saying, 'God, you got the wrong one for this…'

Chapter Two: Living in the Borough of Lackton

"Who shall I say sent me?"

"Are you telling me I am the sent one? Really?"

God told Moses to go to the leadership of the children of Israel to present the plan of leaving Egypt. Moses asked God, who shall he say sent him. God said I AM THAT I AM sent him. I am sure Moses was intently listening for more of an answer, but that was all God gave him.

I AM embodies all that God was, is, and ever will be, all wrapped up in the descriptive name of I AM, the Self-Existent One, the God of Abraham, Isaac, and Jacob. In my creative way of thinking, by that time, Moses' facial expression probably went utterly blank, devoid of any excitement, and positively not thinking anything positive about the plan God was presenting to him. Perhaps you've been there.

"They won't believe me."

"I lack self-confidence."

The conversation continues with more of Moses' concerns. His mind continues to come up with more reasons why God may be incorrect in choosing him to be Israel's leader. He mentally conjured up a scenario of what would happen if he spoke to the elders regarding this freedom plan. What evidence did Moses have to ensure the elders would not believe him? He didn't even go to discuss it with them, and yet he thought he knew what the outcome would be.

God answered by telling him to throw down his staff, which turned into a serpent, then back into a staff again. God then made Moses' hand leprous, white as snow, before returning it to normalcy. He told Moses if they didn't believe the first sign, they would unquestionably believe the second one.

Could this be you?

Oh, you think, getting a business plan together and presenting it to a group of investors sounds ludicrous?

"They're not going to go for this. They wouldn't even consider it. They may not come to the meeting to hear it."

"My credit score is in the toilet. What bank would give me a mortgage to buy a house? Why even try? The number isn't high enough. The bankers will probably laugh about it."

"I don't know why I keep getting ideas to do this when I don't have the time to make it happen. When will I have the time to get that done when I already have so many things on my plate? I am too busy as it is. There is no time for this to happen."

Consider this: If the idea God has enveloped in you keeps gnawing at the walls of your mind, why do you think that is? God does not waste valuable time or thoughts on a person He thinks is not able to perform the task. Moses was mentally so negative. I am sure he didn't consider that God chose him because He was confident Moses could make His idea reality.

"I can't speak well."

"I lack communication skills."

Moses continued by focusing on what he thought he couldn't do. Exodus 4:10 records Moses as telling God that his speech is not eloquent, being slow of speech, having a stammering tongue.

Chapter Two: Living in the Borough of Lackton

God responded by asking Moses a series of questions: Who do you think made the human mouth? And who makes one dumb or deaf, seeing or blind? Is it not I the Lord? Now, therefore, go, as I will be with your mouth, and will teach you what to say. (Exodus 4:11)

God reminded Moses that it is Him who is the Creator of all things, and that includes the mouth. If the mouth is willing to speak, God will put needed words in the speech process of the mouth to communicate the plan. What is interesting is that God told Moses of an impending teachable moment. When God told Moses that he would give him the necessary words, it provided a teaching vehicle that afforded Moses to be a successful student of God's school of action. Are you willing to let go of what you think you can't do, and instead trust God and learn the process of how to do life in a fresh new way?

It didn't seem to be so for Moses, as he had one last protest to present to God. Perhaps the conversation was causing Moses to experience frustration because his excuses weren't changing God's mind. Whatever explanation Moses gave to get out of being God's chosen leader wasn't going over well, yet he tried one last statement. The Message Bible records this last request from Moses as one that seemed to be full of emotion in his voice in Exodus 4:13:

"Oh, Master, please! Send somebody else!"

"This is too much for me to handle! Too little skill, too much responsibility!"

The Bible describes by that time that God got a bit angry with Moses. Yet, it seemed God was willing to offer some assistance in the form of having the Levite, Aaron, to aid Moses with the speaking element. God provided Aaron to be Moses' mouthpiece in speaking to Israel's elders, but it was Moses who told Aaron what to say, as God gave Moses the specific words to tell Aaron. Teaching moments were all around!

So, Moses was not released from his responsibility as he had hoped. He was still under the teaching element of the leadership process while he taught his assistant, Aaron, the same. The last go-round of discord seemed to satisfy Moses. The conversation ended, with Moses taking the staff that God reminded him to take and making his way to his father-in-law, Jethro, to inform him of his plan to return to Egypt. Jethro accepted by telling him to go in peace.

Notice how paramount it was for Moses to petition God for help. Learn from him regarding asking for help and accepting wise counsel from trusted persons. Think of who your trusted group could be for counsel.

Maybe Moses would have been content doing work for his father-in-law for another forty years while raising his family with his wife, Zipporah, and internally experiencing pangs of concern regarding his enslaved people in Egypt. Couple that with thinking, he may not be able to go back, feeling incapable of helping them because of the fear of being thrown in jail for murdering an Egyptian.

You may not have killed anyone (let's hope not!), but you may have a criminal record that you think may prevent you from obtaining a well-paying job. You may be up-to-date this month with paying bills, but there may have been many months before when you weren't. You might think that your past latenesses may prevent you from getting the home of your dreams.

Maybe it has been years, decades, even, since you have touched, let alone opened and read a textbook. During those

Chapter Two: Living in the Borough of Lackton

same years, possibly, you longed to go back to school and finish a GED, a college degree, or start grad school. Time, you *think,* has quickly gone as you have gotten older, and you *think* it can't happen. What happens when this thought process is left running rampant?

The problem with this process is it does nothing for progress. If there is an idea with which we can utilize our God-given gift, one would think it exists for a reason: to *act upon it* (the **A** of **IDEA**, defined in the last chapter). If that is the case, then why not move from an idea to the realm of reality? Perhaps it is in part based on what has happened in our past that aids us in creating the vault and thus keeping us from reaching the destiny God wants for us. The reaction can be the following in the Moses type of mentality:

Indecision

The prefix *in-* according to the Oxford English dictionary means *not*. So, if one is not decisive, one is lacking a decision. The prefix *in-* is not as strong in definition when compared to the prefix *un*. Let's link this prefix with the word certainty.

A close friend of indecision is uncertainty. If being certain denotes a firmness of something that is relied on, *un*certainty takes away that confidence and reliance. Certainty's power decreases when the prefix *un* attaches to it. When *in-* and *un-* prefixes are linked up to thoughts, no wonder there is a lack of movement:

"I'm incapable of meeting this goal."

"I'm inadequate."

"I'm unacceptable. "

"I'm unsure I can do this."

No Solutions

The thought of indecision has a pal named No Solution. If indecision exists, there is no solution as to how the idea could move to the realm of reality.

Mental Replay

Where there is indecisiveness, the mind keeps rehearsing the same problem over and over. The what-ifs keep circling in the brain waves, and it can become endless because there is no solution.

No Peace

The constant turning of wheels internally causes no peace. While you may consider the idea to be a rather good one (which is why it was honored to be tucked away in Vault, to begin with), it causes inner turmoil because it is untouched.

Nothing Getting Accomplished

The total of these non-actions leads to nothing getting accomplished. Thus, stagnancy, inactivity, and other negative hindrances attribute to standing still, impeding the desire to travel at the speed of thought.

Living in Lackton causes indecisiveness, with no conclusions made, coupled with inner conflict. Moving out of Lackton enables one to move and to move forward to making the idea become a reality.

Chapter Two: Living in the Borough of Lackton

Chapter Summary:

1. A Moses Mentality highlights perceived inadequacies.
2. When faced with doing something different, it's easy to formulate excuses to do otherwise.
3. The Moses Mentality usually manifests as indecision, no solutions, mental replay, no peace, and nothing getting accomplished.
4. It's ok to talk with God, telling Him honestly about your ideas and your reservations, but that doesn't mean that he'll abort your mission.

Chapter Three
The Status of Staticus

Sometimes the closer one gets to a breakthrough, the more challenging it becomes. Experiencing change can make the travel to reality seem endless miles away. Yet, at the same time, one is inches away from that explosion of newness. Making the first step is everything, though it can be difficult.

For example, when I wake up in the morning, I may have to stand still for a few moments to 'get the blood moving' through my lower half. It is as though my body decides to inform other parts of me to move forward. Often, I don't have to wait long, as my bladder tells all of me to wobble to the bathroom quickly. There are times when my body does not like to respond to move (particularly my knees), devoid of any walking normalcy, walking like a human cardboard cutout. My knees desire not to bend, and I feel unable to move from the waist down. Once warmed up, my gait eventually gets better, but not at first.

The ideas that live in Staticus suffer from a stagnant rigidity with no action, not flourishing as a lively, vivid thought. The ideas exist, but with no movement, living in the stiffness of a life outside of reality. Though conceived and surviving in the mind, it is devoid of the plan of action. Once thought to be novel, new and original, it is now living like a cardboard cutout, lacking any electrical charge of imagination. The idea, wanting to be alive and moving in a combustible state of visionary purpose, is being forced to be in a state of immobility. It becomes, in Staticus, a pointless mass of conscious inactivity.

Hebrews 12:1 speaks of laying aside every weight that easily besets, or hinders us. When the idea becomes entangled in an area of the mind where there is no action, the idea becomes an unwanted weight, causing pressure to be born, coupled with stress, and as stated earlier, nothing gets accomplished.

What is the definition of the weight? Is it the idea itself, or is it the inaction of the concept? It may be a bit of both. Maybe one is looking at an idea all wrong, feeling the weight that comes with that line of thinking.

If an idea comes with weight, rather than looking at it from a negative standpoint, consider the following Weight within an idea:

Wanting its **E**nergy to **I**gnite to a **G**reater **H**eightened **T**hought!

I think an idea comes packed with energy. When an idea pops into your head, doesn't it make you excited? Don't you, at some point, ponder the thought, 'that's a good idea'? Don't you then perk up to thinking about how that idea could happen? That's the energy having its way with you. And the more you further the plan, the more involved the thoughts become, taking the idea to another heightened level of possibility.

When the mind first conceives an idea, it may cause excitement, thinking it's a great thing to do. But then comes the barrage of questions:

- How is this going to get done?
- How much time will it take to accomplish it?
- How can someone like me do this?

Chapter Three: The Status of Staticus

Sound familiar? It sounds like that is what Moses thought and said to God when presented with the idea of being the leader of Israel to get them to the Promised Land. The problem was that God would not allow His purpose to become inactive. Moses had to experience the weight of the task with all its various components, moving it to reality, and accomplishing the goal God set before him. Have you experienced something like this in any area of your life?

Entrapment

To have an idea that becomes entrapped in Staticus is detrimental to the owner of the plan. The definition of being static is a lack of change and movement or is like an annoying hissing sound (like static on a phone line). If that depicts your idea, it is living in Staticus.

Here's another problem: Staticus is not far from ATAP; why is that? Imagine Staticus as a place chock full of corners, and in this context, it's where ideas gather and talk. Just like you see friends getting together to have a conversation, laugh and joke around, the same thing is happening on many corners of Staticus. Let's imagine being in the central area of Staticus, at the street intersection.

On one corner is a street called Same. Intersecting that street is an avenue called Change. Change Avenue is a long stretch of road that eventually leads ideas out of Staticus. Same Street is the crowded side of the intersection, with numerous ideas talking about the hope of becoming alive, the main sentiment of the ideas. They want to do something, but a force is keeping them from coming alive, such as the forces of fear, doubt, or inability. These and many other negative thought processes in one's mind stagnate the ideas.

They walk like the living dead: being able to breathe somewhat, but not much else. There is no creative nourishment to feast upon, and the ideas feel like they are starving, looking for the food of active creativity. As the business plan links up with a computer software idea on Same Street, they compare their woes of what life would be like after moving from that street.

On the contrary, Change Avenue does not have many ideas that venture to its side. It appears to be a quiet place in the area, yet prides itself on being a passageway where ideas can come and experience metamorphic transformation. Excitement is available on this road. Creativity soars, having a driving force beyond the speeding limit, being able to move out of Staticus quickly. It is full of the willingness to venture to another realm, welcoming the process of movement. Change is winding, full of curbs, and turns. Along the way, the idea transfigures from the dullness of mundanity to the vibrancy of being alive. It is a thriving resident in the realm of reality if only allowed to do so.

When creating this book, there came a period when I slowly came to a stop. What I wanted to do seemed to be the very thing I was fighting against. The inner war I was experiencing was quite subtle, similar to starting at a quick pace, like running…jogging…walking…standing…taking a seat. It was never my intention to end the creativity I knew God had gifted me permanently. Yet, at the same time, I allowed the negativity that was lounging in my past to come front and center, disabling me to depart from Change Avenue and re-enter the mundane personality of Same Street. I eventually realized that wasn't something that I wanted to happen, and as these pages testify, I forged on to complete this book. I had to reverse the subtle changes that led me to put a halt to writing my book from taking a seat… standing… walking… jogging… and eventually running past the finish line.

Chapter Three: The Status of Staticus

"For any movement to gain momentum, it must start with a small action." **Adam Braun**

Staticus has the same weather forecast, and the ideas are always (unhappily I might add) enveloped in an atmosphere of the unknown (known as fog). We all know that fog can occur early in the morning, and when driving on the roads, it can be hard to see what is in front of you. The atmosphere is thick, similar to the adage of 'not seeing the light at the end of the tunnel,' wanting the fog to lift to see everything that surrounds you. However, this never seems to occur. Being in the density of fog does not allow the idea to take shape and thus has no other option but to stand still.

Think of a situation when it was difficult to see the light of a solution. Many owners of ideas think that the thought of standing still is the right solution. After all, aren't we to stand still and see the salvation of God, as the Bible states on more than one occasion? The Bible records God telling the children of Israel that when there were three groups of soldiers on their way with the expressed goal of annihilating them. The word of God states in II Chronicles 20:17:

"Ye shall not need to fight in this battle: set yourselves, stand ye still, and see the salvation of the LORD with you, O Judah and Jerusalem: fear not, nor be dismayed; tomorrow go out against them: for the LORD will be with you."

Even Moses told the people something similar in Exodus 14:13:

"And Moses said unto the people, Fear ye not, stand still, and see the salvation of the LORD, which he will shew to you to day: for the Egyptians whom you have sent to day, ye shall see them again no more forever."

These are just two of many examples where the words stand still appear. So, one may think that living in a mental town where everything is static seems acceptable, like God has rubber-stamped such action.

I get the argument. It's just not the right place to live, and not a place where happiness can live comfortably. Here is an example of standing still from a different vantage point:

Found in II Chronicles 20, King Jehoshaphat got word that groups of armies were on their way to battle against them. That news was not the type of communication anyone, particularly a leader, wanted to hear. The king was only human, and the Bible says his first reaction was fear. One army on their way to wage war against him with the explicit goal of killing him and those under his rulership was bad enough, let alone three groups. It would be understandable for someone receiving that news to want nothing but to hide under their bed covers and pretend to disappear. But in this instance, King Jehoshaphat did anything but remain still. Instead, he sought the Lord, called a fast across the land, and gathered the people together. In prayer, he admitted he did not know what to do other than to set his eyes on God. Imagine the people standing there with their families quietly standing in the stillness of the gathering, and the answer came from God:

"Ye need not fight in this battle; stand still, see My salvation. Don't be scared or dismayed, but go out tomorrow, for I will be with you"
(II Chronicles 20:17).

The next day the Israeli army put their battle gear on, and the king said something rather odd: he commanded the singers to man the front line and sing praises of the Lord, that His mercy endures forever. As a result, many groups of the

Chapter Three: The Status of Staticus

enemy killed each other; all Israel had to do was go out and watch it all unfold, and they *stood still*.

The point is this. What if the king pulled the covers over his head, stayed in bed, and remained still? The outcome would have been ever so different. But King Jehoshaphat moved on many levels, the people backed him up, and everyone took the act of *standing still* to another level.

So, what am I saying here? King Jehoshaphat, having heard the startling news of armies coming with the intent of killing his people, did not stand still. His definition of standing still was shown in his *action*. Doesn't this sound like the terms standing still and action colliding? What is this new definition of action while standing still? Moses had to tell Israel, who were on their way to the Red Sea, a similar proclamation. He said for them not to be afraid, to stand still and see God's salvation regarding the Egyptians, declaring that God would fight for them as they held their peace. They had to learn to *stand still through movement*. They had to move to get in front of the enemy, and once there, they stood still. For your idea to go beyond Staticus, there must be the movement of standing still.

Now, this is quite a different definition of the literal term of standing still, the comment of "I'm just waiting on God to give the go-ahead" type of thinking. Many may say they are waiting on God's response, and they have been waiting for decades for this go-ahead signal to happen. I am not saying to run with the idea without God's guidance. But as written in the first chapter, one can obtain an idea and not go further with it, tucking it away in Vault for safekeeping, with no further movement.

In the biblical examples stated earlier, Moses and King Jehoshaphat did not have time to stand still, but took the time to seek God, and not just get an answer, but *moved and flowed with it*. In this context, they received God's idea and took action. Neither did they go to Staticus; they acted through God's intentions. And isn't that what God gives us, ideas of music, choreography, building design, art and the like? How many ideas do you have that need to be taken from Vault? How many of you need to move while standing still God's way? Can you imagine one bestowed with the gift of singing that never sings? Or how about one with the gift of helping others with starting businesses, but never willing to leave their nine-to-five normality and launch a business of their own?

When looking at a band on stage with the lead singer, I usually look at the backup singers (many of whom can sing better than the 'star'), and I wonder if they ever have the idea of striking it out on their own. I discovered one that took that step.

I watch Elevation Church online weekly and was used to seeing Mack Brock, who had been with the church as a worship leader since the church began, at least the past ten years. In an interview with Christian Post, he spoke of how he was used to being with a team where he could bounce off song ideas with others on the worship team and collaborate in the creation of music. But it seemed God had other plans for Mack, and he resigned from his position at Elevation Church to pursue a solo music career. Talk about moving to Change Avenue! Now, as a solo artist, it was him that had to make the final decision regarding the music. He no longer had the comfort of being surrounded by those he had been with for the past decade. He was stepping out on his own, or was he?

As I read the interview, the word change jumped off of the page, and all that it entails. He described the newness he was experiencing in his life as being a "day-to-day, step by step journey," with his schedule being "uncharted" (the prefix 'un' is a good thing here) while learning how to navigate it all.

Chapter Three: The Status of Staticus

Although it has been an enormous adjustment that appeared scary at times, he used another description of launching out as being a blessing.

What? A blessing? I am sure that the people who are 'waiting on God' are not experiencing blessings in those areas. After all, the blessing comes *after* the God-ordained movement begins. But Mack stated in the interview that once he was *obedient* to God, *that was when* the blessings started coming his way. As of the year of this writing, Mack Brock was on tour, opening for Hillsong Worship, living large on Change Avenue.

Chapter Summary:
1. If your ideas are static and inactive, you are mentally living in Staticus, with your ideas living on Same Street.
2. If you allow your ideas to move to Change Avenue, that means you are choosing not to live like a stiff cardboard cutout that lacks any electrical charge of imagination, allowing the weight of the idea to remain packed with heightened energy.
3. "For any movement to gain momentum, it must start with a small action." Adam Braun
4. Weight could be defined as needless, harassing, or energy that leads to more considerable heightened thought.
5. Waiting on God doesn't mean that you are ceasing all movement.

Chapter Four
The Town of Comfort Zone

What is the comfort that's keeping your idea from moving from the town of Comfort Zone, easing out of Same Street on to Change Avenue, and experiencing the new? I hope you permit yourself to act on what God gave you, to pursue what God is saying is yours…if only you allow yourself to go through the process of working on it.

I thought it would be fitting to talk about what the comfort zone means, so I looked for a dictionary meaning. Of all the definitions I found in the Oxford Dictionary, this is the one I liked best:

A settled method of working that requires little effort and yields barely acceptable results.

A Settled Method

In this context, a settled method is a systematic, organized thought or action of doing something. The technique is an agreed-upon practice that dictates how to carry it out.

Requires Little Effort

The settled method is not complicated and doesn't take a lot of time to do. The word challenge is not part of the technique, because if it takes little effort, it can't be challenging. If it is too hard, it will not qualify under this heading.

Yields Barely Acceptable Results

The return or outcome of the settled method produces next to nothing. Because there is little effort, there is a small accomplishment or yield. Frankly, if one is honest, this type of return is not what one wants, but accepts it nonetheless.

Living in the comfort zone is misleading. While it appears on the surface to be an excellent way to live, it is just the opposite.

Imagine going through life experiencing the ordinary. Living like this requires little effort. Living in the town of Comfort Zone causes one to continue living in the mundane. It leaves no room for growth. Niklas Goeke stated, "The comfort zone is a beautiful place, nothing ever grows there." Therefore, the stagnant stench of non-movement resides. And why would living this way involve movement, when one thinks the comfort zone is the best way to live?

When one is used to the familiar, even if it is not a good thing or place to be, the same actions coupled with similar results keep recurring, because there is an elephant in the room one does not want to deal with, let alone resolve. As I reflect on a few examples from my life, two stand out.

At one point, I stayed at one church long after I knew I was supposed to move on. I served there some twenty-six plus years, being heavily involved in the music ministry, and from time to time teaching Bible classes. God kept tugging at my heart that it was time to move, but I didn't want to. I was fearful of the unknown. I accepted the life of being in the comfort zone: everyone knew me, and I was familiar with the responsibilities of being a leader within the music ministry. But something kept nagging at me that there must be more. Even though I was active, at the same time, I was comfortable. The time came when I had to make a move that involved

Chapter Four: The Town of Comfort Zone

leaving that church. It was one of the hardest decisions I had to make, but I knew it was something that I had to do.

Another place where I felt I overstayed my time was at my job. I believe that the time that I stayed there far exceeded my extended stay at the church. I felt God was telling me it was time to go, even saying I would not get another job with that employer. After applying to over forty vacancies and not getting offered anything, I decided it was time to leave by way of retirement.

The problem was that I'd never done this retirement thing before, so I had nothing to rely upon. My main fear was I would not be financially stable enough to pay all my bills. Hundreds of times, I did the numbers, probably in hopes of seeing there was a mistake, and I had to continue living in the comfort zone of working a job that no longer fulfilled me. Despite my wishful thinking, I knew that I needed to move to a new stage of life.

Fast forward with the Moses story. After finally leaving Egypt, Israel was well on their way to the land God prepared for them, described as flowing with milk and honey. Through the command of God, Moses gathered twelve men to spy on the Promised Land, to bring back fruit as evidence, and present a report describing the land and the people who lived there.

The men brought their report to Moses and Aaron, and all of Israel. A summary of that report to Israel was the following:

"Yes, we went to the land you told us to view, and surely, it is a great land that flows with milk and honey. Just look at this fruit! It is magnificent!"
(Numbers 13:27)

However, they also said that the people that live there were strong and the cities were walled and great. The thirtieth verse of Numbers 13 recorded that Caleb stilled the people before he said,

> *"Let us go up at once, and possess it: for we are well able to overcome it."*

Caleb was one of the spies, so he saw the same things the others viewed, yet he was confident that victory would prevail. He was prepared to do whatever was needed to make change happen and obtain God's blessing.

The other men in the spy group were not so willing. They responded that the people they saw in the land were more robust and that Israel was not able to possess the land. They further stated that the land "eats up" the people that live there, and as a result, they are "men of great stature."

Numbers 14:1 defines Israel as being distraught to the point they cried through the night and complained about Moses and Aaron. They commented that they came that far only to die, with their families being prey. Their solution was to get a leader who could get them back to Egypt.

Initially, the children of Israel wanted out of Egypt, yearning to move from the daily back-breaking work under Pharoah, crying out to the Lord to provide a solution, and they were eager to move to the land He prepared for them. Yet there was a turnaround of thinking that perhaps going back to Egypt would not be that bad after all. They remembered eating; Egypt had good food. Egypt was comfortable. While in Egypt, they were not the nomadic people they presently were, wandering from place to place, setting up their tents only to break them down to move to another area.

Chapter Four: The Town of Comfort Zone

Ever been so close to success yet, at the same time, be willing to accept the mediocrity of going back to the way things were? Have you ever been willing to take the humdrum existence of living average? But at the same time (and if you are honest with yourself), do you sense deep down that change is the God-given prescription you need to come *alive*? God says,

"Behold, I will do a new thing; now it shall spring forth; shall ye not know it? I will even make a way in the wilderness and rivers in the desert" (Isaiah 43:19).

Isn't this different than living the mundane? This verse has no content about living average, or daily living the same while accepting a lower standard. It is quite the opposite!

What happens when you choose to eliminate the comforts that tend to stop you in your tracks of moving forward?

The campaign of an **IDEA** (**I**ndividual **D**esign that's **E**nacted by some sort of **A**ctivity or action, presented in the first chapter) can be born within the developing trust of the process. So, trust the process. But what if the process is not something you want to experience? What can you do to change that thought process? It's all in this: accepting the challenge. What does that mean?

Your idea of going back to school, for example, might be met with challenges. The challenge of picking a school, should it be online or not, looking at the finances that may include getting school loans, creating the time to attend class, and doing the work, which may require not meeting up with friends after work or on the weekends. Imagine going to grad school, applying for and getting accepted, and *then* finding out you will be a first-time dad to not one, but twins! What a challenge that is!

This challenge was real for my son, Stephen. I am sure his head was spinning like a top concerning how to complete school while going to work and taking care of his twin boys, never being in such a position, and not have the experience to fall back on. What an overwhelming challenge that could be. But he decided to flow with it all, making sure he was at all the doctor appointments with his partner, Angela, showing his support to her, buying Philadelphia Eagles onesies, and other more needed items. As I worked on completing this book, my grandsons, Josiah and Elijah, made their entrances into the world!

So how is a challenge met? You meet the problem by choosing to do so. Moses decided to follow God despite his concerns. King Jehosophat decided to move while standing still. My son, Steve, braved the movement of continuing through the unknown territory of being a father.

Living in the Town of Comfort Zone requires little effort, a settled method of working that yields minimum results of living life. These results happen if you refuse to address the comforts that hold you back.

Chapter Four: The Town of Comfort Zone

Chapter Summary:

1. By definition, a comfort zone is a settled method of working that requires little effort and yields barely acceptable results.
2. It may be familiar, but growth doesn't happen in the town of Comfort Zones.
3. The comfort zone can tempt you to return to inferior places and situations.
4. The best solution to moving forward is to accept the challenge and step outside of your comfort zone.

Chapter Five
The Town of Fearford

Moving from idea to reality is a great work, and in the process, you experience a newness of life. But newness can come with stressors. Stressors can cause a strain on what you are trying to accomplish. The tension between what you want to obtain and getting to the goal line can be one of anguish, and while there are many, the focus will be on the stressor of fear.

Fear is a Perception

Fear is full of possibilities and not good ones. It causes anxiety, thinking something wrong will happen, without the support or proof that something of dread will happen. Think of an instance that you just knew deep inside something terrible was going to happen, but it never occurred. According to the Oxford Dictionary of English, perception is an awareness of something, the way in which it is regarded, understood, and interpreted. I like the word interpreted as it hones in on how one thinks something to be. Things can be interpreted in a particularly cynical or optimistic manner. One way to explain fear is:

False Evidence Appearing Real

When something is false, it is the opposite of being factual. Evidence is proof that something exists. When something appears real, it could very well be an illusion. Those illusions impact our perceptions, which influence our declarations and decisions. As I was writing this, an example from my childhood popped up in my memory bank.

At the time, I had just started a new school in Philadelphia (moving from Indianapolis, Indiana); I was in the third grade. It was recess at school, and all the kids were outside playing. Before I knew it, I was at the center of the schoolyard. Everything seemed to stop when one of the girls said she was going to fight me after school; I was so scared. What did I do to get this? As the day went on, the more fearful I became. The fight happened after school, and though we were on the sidewalk, we were surrounded by a human fighting ring, as the crowd of kids circled my opponent and me.

I remember my father had just bought me a new winter coat, and I wore it on that day. The iron fence my opponent was bouncing me off of had been painted black earlier in the day and had not dried. So, as the girl was smacking me around, the human boxing ring opened. The girl started throwing me against the painted fence, and my new coat was getting plummeted with black paint. When I got home, crying, and my jacket ruined, my father walked me back to school. We spoke to the principal, and I told her everything that happened.

The girl was punished, and when we had a meeting later with her and her parents, she kept saying I started it by hitting her first. My response with all my might (and my swollen face), was that she was wrong.

Fast forward two years from that day. I don't know why, but while I was in the bathroom of my grandmother's home (back in Indianapolis), that incident popped back in my mind, recalling what happened, and guess what? The girl was right. I did hit her during recess. But it was to play tag, not to cause a fight.

Chapter Five: The Town of Fearford

Though I firmly believed that I had evidence that she started the fight, there were misinterpretations and misunderstandings. At the time, I felt the other girl hit me first, but it was me who began by striking her first. What I thought to be accurate and appeared to be real for years was false. I'm not the only one that is affected by fear.

Many entertainers suffer from fear, though they have the talent and have been successful for decades, and yet, they continue to deal with that issue. Award-winning singer and actress Barbara Streisand's stage fright comes to mind. I do not believe that for the *individual,* fear is not real. To the one who experiences it, it is indeed real. Earlier in the book, I described how I stayed stuck in a job I did not particularly like, but because of fear that there was nothing else in the job world, I remained in the same position for years.

When faced with a situation, we have two ways that we can approach them. We can choose to filter our circumstances through fear or faith. Let's compare and contrast fear and faith.

Fear	**Faith**
A belief system	A belief system
Dread and suspicion	Confidence and conviction
Negative	Positive
Mistrust	Trust
Now fear lacks evidence of what we're afraid of; it has no underbelly but is full of dread and terribleness without evidence of truth.	"Now faith is the substance of things hoped for, the evidence of things not seen" (Hebrews 11:1).
Perception-based	Evidence-based

Courage Fights in the Face of Fear

To get out of Fearford and move to ATAP, AW, one needs to develop acts based on evidence despite danger or disapproval. A famous biblical story is found in the third chapter of Daniel. There was a showdown between King Nebuchadnezzar and three Hebrew boys whose parents named them Shadrach, Meshach, and Abed-Nego. The king wanted everyone to bow before a gold image he set up, or be thrown in the fiery furnace. Shadrach, Meshach, and Abed-Nego refused to do so. When the king heard this from others, he became incensed and had the boys come before him. The boys boldly stated before everyone that they would not do what the king decreed, saying that if they had to go to the fiery furnace, so be it. They stated, "God is able to deliver us from the fiery furnace, and He will deliver us from your hand, O king"(Daniel 3:17). They further said that even if God did not deliver them from the furnace, they would not serve the king's gods. Now it was on!

King Nebuchadnezzar got so angry at the response that he not only ordered the Hebrew boys to be thrown into the furnace, he ordered the temperature to be turned up seven times, to the point that the soldier who was to open the door got burned to a crisp because of the high heat! Once the boys were thrown into the furnace, King Nebuchadnezzar saw something strange. He was confused, as he noticed there were four people in the oven. He confirmed with others that only three were thrown in. When all was said and done, the king acknowledged that the fourth person looked like the son of God. The Hebrew boys, bound and thrown into the furnace, came out not smelling like smoke, their clothes were not burned, and there were no bodily injuries. Then King Nebuchadnezzar, once adamant about everyone bowing to the golden image, now said that those that did not honor the

Chapter Five: The Town of Fearford

God of Shadrach, Meshach, and Abed-Nego would be cut to pieces, and their bones burned. What a change of events that took place! And it was all because the Hebrew boys dared to face King Nebuchadnezzar.

The Bible does not address if the Hebrew boys were afraid, but they were human, and it could be that at some point, they had to face fear. They made a statement that you don't often hear in sermons. When King Nebuchadnezzar asked, "And who is the god who will deliver you from my hands?" (Daniel 3:15) their answer was, "O Nebuchadnezzar, we have no need to answer you in this matter" (Daniel 3:16). They didn't even deal with his question. Instead, they took a stand through their statement of not bowing to the golden image. They fought the king with faith and courage.

No doubt, there was an atmosphere of fear enveloped around the Hebrew boys. Just like the kids who were surrounding me and the girl who fought me after school, the people of the community were surrounding the boys who were facing King Nebuchadnezzar, and they needed to make a decision. The moral conviction Shadrach, Meshach, and Abed-Nego exhibited against the possible death was courage in action, wrapped around the belief system of faith. Courage was the knock-out punch that made them conclude that regardless of what happened, they had confidence that their God would come to their aid.

When faith is in action, fear (false evidence appearing real) has to flee. When there is confidence in what one is doing, the substance of faith becomes the evidence. That means if one has the belief system that the idea has been planted deep within, there has to be the faith that the idea will no longer be stuck in their mind, but will be born into reality. It will happen, it will come to pass. The Hebrew boys allowed their faith that was wrapped in courage to speak for them. They stood in the face of annihilation, and let their courage fight, taking a stand against possibilities that never came to fruition. The possibility of death did not win; the belief system of faith and courage sprinkled their lives with a victory. It may also have meant flipping fear upside down.

What is keeping you from being a conqueror of fear? What are the thought processes that are preventing your idea from living in a world of reality? Perhaps changing the acronym of fear may help. Change **F**alse **E**vidence **A**ppearing **R**eal to:

Face It **E**xpose It **A**ssess It **R**elease It

Face It/**E**xpose It – Define what is troubling you; don't deny it. Make it as plain as you can. Think of an instance when you faced fear square in the face, and you won. What key points do you remember that helped you be the victor and not the loser? In regards to making your idea reality, can you apply any of those points now? When you get ready to do something new, what stalls you from making it happen?

Assess It – Is fear who you are? Is fear who you want to be? Is this something you want to continue to struggle with? How has your life been with it? What would your life be without it?

Release It – It is time to let it go.

When fear is viewed from a different perspective (**F**ace It, **E**xpose It, **A**ssess It, **R**elease It), the mind can be exposed to believing an idea can be actualized. A belief system is strengthened when facing the challenge of experiencing the new. The thought process of **FEAR** (**F**alse **E**vidence **A**ppearing **R**eal) eliminates any chance of allowing the idea to become real.

Chapter Five: The Town of Fearford

Chapter Summary:

1. Fear can cause you to think that something negative will happen when there is no evidence to support it.
2. While fear is perception-based, faith is evidence-based.
3. Courage fights in the face of fear.
4. Conquer fear by facing it, exposing it, assessing it, and releasing it.

Chapter Six
Bordering ATAP

ATAP is a place where what seems like the impossible is possible. It is a realm where ideas are free to roam and blossom into the outside world of reality. It is where there is a finishing of the work. The idea is now plumped with the nutrients of the hard work one has put into it that enables it to be birthed.

When you are bordering ATAP, your mentality and actions are drastically different than when you're relaxing in any other city, town, or municipality. You have escaped Vault by refusing to tuck your ideas away. You have risen above from the Borough of Lackton and feeling as if you were unqualified. You have dislodged yourself from Staticus by refusing to remain stuck. You have pressed past the Town of Comfort Zone and chose discomfort to reach your end goal. You have waltzed through the Town of Fearford as you redefined fear and its impact on you. Now, you are just at the cusp of entering All Things Are Possible, Anywhere.

About a month after starting the process of retirement, my son called me one evening and asked if I was still awake. He asked me if I was sitting down. Then he told me that not only was I about to become a grandmother for the first time, but it would be to twins!

For the past four years, I had been a caregiver to my mother, who has dementia. Even though she is being cared for in a nursing home, I realized the disease was progressing.

I continue to gravel with the fact I could not 'fix it' for her, and the guilt that came with putting her in a home mentally remained. I was concerned for the babies who seemed to be causing concern with the doctors to such a degree they moved up the date of their birth, which meant I had to change my travel plans.

Then I noticed something was happening in the physical realm.

It was getting harder and harder to get through the front door of my home. Mail was piled up in many spots; shoes were also piled up in many places near the door; the sofa was beginning to disappear under the coats that had not been hung up; likewise, the dining room table was full of grocery items that had not been put away. Earrings were not in the jewelry box, and when I wanted to wear them, I couldn't find them. Dirty dishes were piled in the sink, and Benny, my cat was meowing at me that he was out of food and water (which I quickly gave, but that happened more than once, despite his constant reminding). At least I washed laundry weekly, but keeping my ironing up to date, that was another matter, so they were partially done.

There is a correlation between the clutter we see and the mental confusion loaded in our brains. Have you seen the television show *Hoarders?* It's about people who live with clutter out of control, but the physical and (on that show) massive piles of stuff denotes a mental issue that needs to be dealt with. Thank God I was not up to that level, but for me, what I observed was a concern.

I noticed the physical clutter was an indication I was mentally out of sync, and this hindered my momentum. Places that were designated for one thing were being transformed to another use, which wasn't good because the new designation was not making my life better. Some things had to be in their

Chapter Six: Bordering ATAP

rightful place. The shoes had to be put away. The coats had to be hung up. The mail had to be sorted through and either discarded or put in files. All of these things were not being done. Instead, I was becoming disorganized physically, which was a representation of my being mentally disorganized and cluttered, living life in chaos, just like my mind was experiencing.

Psychologists have said there is a correlation between the two. It is not so much the stuff that is disorganized, they say; instead, it is the reason it is chaotic in the first place. What was my reason? I believe it was based on life changes: some that had taken place (the sickness of my mother), and others that were on the horizon of becoming a reality (birth of grandchildren and retirement). These current and soon-to-be events were causing me to build piles of stuff that somehow physically represented what I was mentally experiencing. The collections of shoes may express me feeling stuck in my tracts from moving forward because I didn't know what was about to happen. While I admitted to myself, I was about to tread on an untraveled territory, I didn't know how all this was going to work out. I'm the type who wants to know exactly that – how things are going to work out. I guess that's why I like the story of Moses; perhaps we are very much alike, more than I want to admit.

But here is the good part. Once the piles were observed in the physical realm, I became determined to organize my clutter. The mountain of shoes was eventually put away, the coats were hung up (even cleaned!), and the mail is at least being addressed and tossed where needed. Let's say some progress has been made. God can use anything to get a point across, and in this instance, it was a Lifetime Christmas movie (I'm a sucker for watching them).

The two main characters had an issue of living life in their respective comfort zones. He was his father's business partner, and she was an accountant (really, God? You had to make her profession the same as mine?). They both had a passion: him being an artist and her being a designer. In one scene, they spoke of how kids (who he was teaching how to paint), in their naïve way of talking, seem to talk about hope unknowingly. He said they seem to believe, and "maybe that's all that's needed." I turned to an empty chair in my living room (like God was sitting in it) and said, "Really, God?" but in essence, I believe that is what he was encouraging me with, just to believe. At the time, I needed to be reminded of that.

The root of why one struggles with believing runs deep and is full of past failures. But here is a positive indicator of a failure. When I think of something that went awry in my past, what I can take away from it is that I tried to do something for a failure to exist. Have you thought of failures in that context? The problem with failure is it can taint any chances of trying again. Each new day we are gifted with the opportunity to try again. Each day grants us twenty-four hours to create possibilities of trying again. Those hours afford us to think of what went right and how we can stop just nearing the border of ATAP, but enter therein.

I had to make some decisions. Regarding retirement, I set up a financial plan that would enable me to live comfortably. Still, I had to acknowledge and choose to stick to that plan if retirement was to work for me and not be forced to get another job because of impending financial trouble. I changed my travel in anticipation of holding my newborn grandsons. I continued to care for my mom, being a listening ear to her mental struggles. And let's just say the piles of stuff have been addressed, but it continues to be a work in progress.

Chapter Six: Bordering ATAP

I knew I was close to ATAP, and I was mentally touching the border. I was having a challenging time finishing this book. I did not come to a complete stop, but for some reason, I kept putting the completion of it off, like I couldn't do it. Fear was hitting me big time (false evidence appearing real), and not finishing the book was a thought that kept circling in my mind. I thought my idea, so close to being finalized, was not going to make its destination of being real. But am I only talking about the idea being realized and making it happen? I believe there is more to this journey than just the idea being realized and moved to ATAP; I realized I had to not only deal with the realization of the idea but choose to deal with someone also entering ATAP…, *me.*

All **T**hings **A**re **P**ossible, **A**nywhere is a place where anyone can mentally live. It can be described as a way of thinking, a choice of believing that what appears on the surface to be impossible is indeed possible, to those who believe. That is what Jesus said numerous times to people who approached him with a problem. He asked the father who brought his son to him for healing in Mark 9:23, "If you can believe, all things are possible to him who believes." Mark 9:23 is one of my favorite passages, and as you can guess, it's where I got the title for this book. As the two men talk further, the father says, "I believe, but help thou mine unbelief" (Mark 9:24). I think that is where I found myself. The father in the biblical story was very distraught. Part of him believed Jesus was the answer, and the other part of him struggled to believe that Jesus could help. Perhaps you have been there.

The ideas have arrived at a place of peace, not chaos; an atmosphere of recognizing change has occurred. It may have taken months or years, but the change has happened…and that difference is in *you!* How will you know the destination is complete? All this time, I had written about how to move the idea forward, when in actuality, it was me who needed to be content with entering the thought of the possibility of things happening, being actualized. For something to change, I have to believe it to be so. I had to choose to fight the elements that kept me stuck in a Moses Mentality, changing thoughts of inadequacy to the understanding that I could allow the idea to become a reality. I was the combustion that provided the energy to move past Lackton, eliminating the what-if negativity. It had to be me who believed it to be so.

The idea was in me. There were things I had to deal with, from bringing it out of Vault to feed it the nutrients of time, work, and creativity to make the idea robust with complete finality. The idea couldn't become a reality on its own. I had to be strong enough to bring it to realness. At the same time, I had to lift my mind to a level to believe that all this was indeed possible if I could only accept that I had what it took to do it. It is not only the idea entering ATAP. It is the essence of *you* that realizes entrance into the atmosphere of ATAP.

There is an empowerment that begins when something has been completed. It enables you to acknowledge that this actually can be done. What a peace that infiltrates your soul when you can look at your manuscript, your business plan, completed application papers to send to school admission, to sit down with a financial planner who can assist you in getting your debts paid off, and other goals. The possibilities are endless, and that is the beauty of living in ATAP. The realization of beginning the process can happen anywhere, even in your car at night when the frustration of where you are has you considering making changes. Then the time comes to make it happen. That, my friend, is ATAP. When you struggled financially wondering if a thing would ever change, later choosing to do whatever it took to come to the day when you got the shiny new keys that cemented you as a

Chapter Six: Bordering ATAP

homeowner, that's ATAP. When you finish writing a book, send it to the publisher, and contemplate new book ideas, including a screenplay (oh my!), that is genuinely ATAP. Are you ready for the challenge?

What will it take for you to say it's time for a change? When one idea you have wanted to do is finally done, the mental door opens to continue the furtherance toward the horizon. I wish I could assure you that the struggle ends, but I can't; the battle continues, but it will not overpower you as it has in the past. Like me, your journey will be challenging. Similar to my struggle, you have to fight past what you consider normal, and develop new elements of the new in your life. It is time to go beyond the finiteness of the past and towards the infinite future of not only the idea entering ATAP but the faith to believe you can mentally move to the place destined for greatness!

Chapter Summary:

1. Bordering ATAP requires leaving all of the other cities, towns, and municipalities behind.
2. In order to enter ATAP, you have to believe and continue to try again, despite failure.
3. Not only does your idea need to enter ATAP, but *you* do as well.

Chapter Seven
Mind AveNews

This chapter may be the shortest or the most extended section of the book. That is up to you, as it is not the last chapter, but the beginning of new avenues, *written by you*. Everyone discovers their avenues of newness in ways distinct to self, and for this reason, the majority of this chapter is for you, devoid of words. I request you fill in the blanks by allowing ink to flow to paper, creating the words as you feel them, and I hope to guide you to writing your story and creating new *mind avenews*. Don't limit yourself to the space in this book. Perhaps a separate journal would suffice in getting all your thoughts on paper. There are no right answers to these questions, so be as honest as you can as you write about yourself.

Describe yourself. Are you a go-getter, or just the opposite? Define your immediate family and marital status. Are you renting or buying your home? Do you love your job or hate it (or somewhere in between)? What defines You? These are a few probing questions but feel free to dive in as deep as you would like.

_____
_____
_____
_____
_____
_____

ATAP, AW

Chapter Seven: Mind AveNews

What have you always wanted to do? What gets you excited, all warm and fuzzy inside when you think of it?

ATAP, AW

How can you make your idea happen?

Chapter Seven: Mind AveNews

In which cities, towns and municipalities have you been mentally living in?

Within Raef is an area called Vault. Are your fuzzy ideas stored there? Why do you think you store them in Vault? Remember: Ideas won't keep. Something must be done about them.

Chapter Seven: Mind AveNews

What do you feel you are lacking that keeps you mentally living in Lackton?

ATAP, AW

What can you do to change that mindset?

Chapter Seven: Mind AveNews

Are you an 'in' or 'un' person? (See Chapter 2) Why?

Have there been times when you felt you were living on Same Street? What did you need to do to make the move to Change Avenue? If you did, does this seem scary to you? Why or why not?

Chapter Seven: Mind AveNews

"The greatest things in life tend to happen outside our comfort zones, and doubting your ability to step outside of your comfort zone will keep you stuck."
Amy Morin

What do you like most about living in the Town of Comfort Zone? Describe what your life is like when you live in the comfort zone.

_____
_____
_____
_____
_____
_____
_____
_____
_____
_____
_____
_____
_____
_____
_____
_____
_____
_____
_____
_____
_____

"You'll always miss 100% of the shots you don't take."
Wayne Gretzky

Think of a time when you tried something, but it didn't work. Does the remembrance of that failure hinder you from trying something new? Explain.

Chapter Seven: Mind AveNews

List those who can help you bring your idea into reality, and give reasons for your choices.

"Those who lack the courage will always find a philosophy to justify it." **Albert Camus**

Japanese Proverb: *"Fear is only as deep as the mind allows."*

"Courage is doing what you're afraid to do. There can be no courage unless you're scared." World War II United States pilot **Eddie V Rickenbacker**

What do you think about the above quotes? Can you relate to any of them? Jot down some thoughts regarding you and fear.

___
___
___
___
___
___
___
___
___
___
___
___
___
___
___
___
___
___
___
___

Chapter Seven: Mind AveNews

"A good tool improves the way you work. A great tool improves the way you think." **Jeff Duntemann**

What mental tools could you use to propel your idea forward towards ATAP, AW?

ATAP, AW

"Jesus said to him, 'If you can believe, all things are possible to him who believes'" (Mark 9:23 NKJV).

Answering all the questions in this book, put together a statement of what your belief system presently is and what you want it to be in realizing your idea, and residing in ATAP, AW.

_____
_____
_____
_____
_____
_____
_____
_____
_____
_____
_____
_____
_____
_____
_____
_____
_____
_____
_____
_____
_____
_____

You are on your way, my friend, to ATAP, AW (**A**ll **T**hings **A**re **P**ossible, **A**ny**w**here). Don't merely visit. Reside there forever.

About the Author

Debra Cox, an avid writer and new author fell in love with writing as a teenager. From high school teachers to college professors, Debra was constantly encouraged to pursue her gift and passion of writing. Whether writing for pure enjoyment or creating newsletters for organizations, Debra is sure to incorporate an uplifting faith-based word of encouragement.

Debra received her Masters of Theological Studies from Palmer Theological Seminary in 2016. She is the creator of lucidity2015.com, a blog that captures the journey, joys, and challenges of being a caregiver and strengthenize.com, a blog whose purpose is to spread faith-based encouragement with the world.

Debra Cox is the mother of, Stephen, who motivated her to actualize her dream of becoming a published author.

**Follow Debra's blogs at
lucidity2015.com and strengthenize.com.**

www.ingramcontent.com/pod-product-compliance
Lightning Source LLC
LaVergne TN
LVHW091317080426
835510LV00007B/521